AIR
SICK
HUMOR

by
William K. Joric, Ph.D.
Pilot

O&A, Inc.
Prepared/Published in USA

ABOUT THE AUTHOR . . .

William K. Joric, Ph.D., is the author and publisher of over 30 technical publications. An educator, a military and current civilian pilot with over 5,000 flying hours, Bill also spends a huge amount of his time flying on the airlines. Combine this with his 30 years of marriage to a former flight attendant, and his interest in humorous stories related to travel by air is obvious.

DEDICATION

This book is dedicated to the thousands of airline professionals who deal daily with the sort of organized insanity that is modern air travel. Considering all the hassled, angry, rude, and downright nutty passengers these folks work with every day, you'll probably agree that they do their jobs with an uncommon amount of patience, good humor, and professionalism. For efforts which keep us all flying, and for their contributions, without which this book would not be possible, thanks.

INTRODUCTION

This is a collection of true stories dealing with flying, as related to us by pilots, flight attendants, gate agents, reservvation agents and passengers. While some of them may sound improbable, remember the old saying, "Truth is stranger than fiction." If you still have doubts, ask anyone who works for an airline. They'll likely have some tales that will top those you'll see here.

CHAPTERS

The Reservation

An inside view of the trials and tribulations of an airline reservationist, plus some selected travel agent experiences.

The Airport

Airline employees often think that passengers check their brain at the curb when departing. And, they don't retrieve their brain until they land at their final destination. A funny collection of airport stories relayed by sky caps, customer service agents, ramp personnel and . . . passengers.

The Flight

Okay . . . you're on board. No problems now. WRONG! The pilots and flight attendants take their turn telling their on-board stories.

Turbulence

The final chapter describes some of the funniest additional stories associated with the airline industry.

It should come as no surprise that the airlines receive complaints . . . lots of complaints. While many of them are probably well founded, they also get some like these.

Res 1

Common complaints:

- Arriving too early
- Charging more for a ticket than was paid on the previous trip . . . several years before
- Sitting next to a passenger who hogged the armrest
- Flight attendants weren't attractive enough

Res 2

Exit row seating is designed with more room for easier egress in case of an emergency. It's probably a compliment to the airlines' safety record that most passengers only think about the fact that these rows offer more leg room. The exit row has become nearly as desirable as first class. The creative reasons callers use for insisting on the exit row can defy the imagination. A broken leg is the most common reason given, even though it's obvious that the cast would prevent the passenger from performing emergency duties should they be required, and likely block other passengers from getting to the exit. When told this, one passenger offered to remove his cast for the duration of the flight.

Res 3
The most creative may be the man who told an agent (without laughing) that he had a strange ailment called "stretch-leg-itis" which required him to keep his legs fully extended, necessitating the exit row.

Res 4
Requesting a seat on an over-sold flight, a woman was told that she could be put on the "wait list". The obviously confused woman was concerned that she might weigh too much to make it onto the flight.

Res 5
A woman called reservations to inquire if the airline flew to Walt Disney World. The agent couldn't resist replying, "Oh, yes, ma'am. And a pretty big city it is, too."

Res 6
A man called reservations to express his displeasure at the restrictions imposed by the Wright Amendment. This law prohibits travel from Dallas' Love Field to any airport not in a state bordering Texas, with an exception for Alabama and Mississippi. The man complained, "Well, California

is right next to Texas, so why can't I go from Dallas to Los Angeles?"

Res 7
A client called in inquiring about a flight package to Hawaii. After going over all the cost info, she asked, "would it be cheaper to fly to California and then take the train to Hawaii?"

Res 8
I got a call from a woman who wanted to go to Capetown. I started to explain the length of the flight and the passport information then she interrupted me with, "I'm not trying to make you look stupid, but Capetown is in Massachusetts." Without trying to make her look like the stupid one, I calmly explained, "Cape Cod is in Massachusetts, Capetown is in South Africa." Her response . . . "click."

Res 9
A secretary called in looking for a hotel in Los Angeles. She gave me various names off a list, none of which I could find. I finally had her fax me the list. To my surprise, it was a list of hotels in New Orleans, Louisiana. She thought the LA stood for Los Angeles, and that New Orleans was a suburb of LA. Worst of all, when I called her back, she was not even embarrassed.

Res 10

A man called, furious about a Florida package we did. I asked what was wrong with the vacation in Orlando. He said he was expecting an ocean-view room. I tried to explain that is not possible, since Orlando is in the middle of the state. He replied, "Don't lie to me. I looked on the map and Florida is a very thin state."

Res 11

I got a call from a man who asked, "Is it possible to see England from Canada?" I replied, "No." He said, "But they look so close on the map."

Res 12

Another man called and asked if he could rent a car in Dallas. When I pulled up the reservation, I noticed he had a 1-hour lay-over in Dallas. I asked him why he wanted to rent a car and he said, "I heard Dallas was a big airport, and I need a car to drive between the gates to save time."

Res 13

A nice lady just called. She needed to know how it was possible that her flight from Detroit left at 8:20 am and got into Chicago at 8:33 am. I tried to explain that Michigan was an hour ahead of Illinois, but she could not understand the concept of time zones. Finally I told her the plane went very fast, and she bought that!

A woman called and asked, "Do airlines put your physical description on your bag so they know whose luggage belongs to who?" I said, "No, why do you ask?" She replied, "Well, when I checked in with the airline, they put a tag on my luggage that said FAT and I'm overweight. Is there any connection?" After putting her on hold for a minute while I "looked into it" (I was actually laughing), I came back and explained the city code for Fresno is FAT, and that the airline was just putting a destination tag on her luggage.

Res 15

I just got off the phone with a man who asked, "How do I know which plane to get on?" I asked him what exactly he meant, to which he replied, "I was told my flight number is 823, but none of these damn planes have numbers on them."

Res 16

A woman called and said, "I need to fly to Pepsi-cola on one of those computer planes." I asked if she meant to fly to Pensacola on a commuter plane." She said, "Yeah, whatever."

Res 17

A business man called and had a question about the documents he needed in order to fly to China. After a lengthy discussion about passports, I reminded him he needed a visa. "Oh no I don't. I've been to China many times and never had to have one of those." I double checked and sure enough, his stay required a visa. When I told him this he said, "Look, I've been to China four times and every time they have accepted my American Express."

Res 18

A travel agent got a call from an irate customer who didn't like his seat assignment. He continued to complain, and ended up by saying, "Besides, the flight's almost empty!" After a pause, the agent asked, "Sir, are you on board?" "Yes", he replied, "I am calling you on the Airphone", sounding even more annoyed. Thinking quickly, the agent asked, "Sir, do you see an open seat that you like better?" When the customer replied that there was an open exit row aisle seat at 19C, she told him, "Just go ahead and take that seat. I'll make the change for you in the computer right now!"

Several reservation agents report that callers always assume they're talking to someone in their own city when, in fact,, they may be speaking with an agent anywhere in the country.

Res 19
One caller was sure that the agent was being difficult when she asked for the departure city. "Here", answered the caller.

"All right, departing from 'Here' and you'll be traveling to what city?"

Now sure that she was being made fun of, the passenger replied, "There.".

Without the slightest hesitation, the agent intoned, "Will that be round trip or one way from Here to There?"

Res 20
Agent: Hello, BigBuck Airlines, this is Scott. May I help you?
Pass: Yes, I need to leave here on the 14th, or

13

the 13th, depending on the fare, and I'll
want to return on the 24th or 25th .

Agent: Excuse me ma'am . . .

Pass: Young man, don't interrupt! As I was
saying, I'll return from either Milwaukee
or Chicago on the 24th or 25th.

Agent: Ahh, now we're getting somewhere.

Pass: Excuse me?

Agent: Well, now I at least know where you're
going. Would you mind letting me know
where you're departing from?

Pass: You mean you're not here in Gunnison?

Agent: No, ma'am, I'm in Los Angeles. So,
you're leaving Gunnison on the 13th or
14th and returning from either Milwaukee
or Chicago on the 24th or 25th . . . right?

Pass: No, I'm sorry, I'll really be leaving from
Billings, Montana.

Agent: No problem. Now if we can decide on the
dates, we'll be in business.

Pass: By the way, this will be non-stop won't it?
I don't want to change planes.

Agent: (Barely containing laughter) No, ma'am,
there are no non-stops from Billings to
Milwaukee or Chicago, but if you're going
to Milwaukee, we offer convenient
connections through Denver and Chicago.

Pass: Convenient? That's 3 airplanes each way!

Agent: Yes, ma'am, but think of it. That's 6
airplanes for only $693.00.

Pass: (Now laughing) What a deal, 6 airplanes

for only $700! That's what you call "convenient connections"?

Agent: Yes, ma'am. I get paid to say that.

Res 21

Another woman called wanting to fly from "here to Kansas City". When the agent asked the obvious questions, "Where are you?", the caller replied acidly, "At my kitchen sink!"

Res 22

A reservations agent tells of the call she was taking when the caller became ill. The sounds of someone becoming physically sick did little for the agent's digestion, but she gamely held on until the caller returned to the line. Apologizing, the lady said she wasn't sure what was wrong, but thought the large bag of "M&M's" she'd just eaten weren't agreeing with her. They continued with the reservation and were nearly done when the woman became violently ill once again. Controlling her own nausea, the agent again waited until the woman could talk and completed the call.

At that point, the agent took a much deserved break and left her position without knowing that the call had been monitored by a training class in progress. When she returned from her break, she found a gift on her computer . . . a large bag of "M&M's", donated by a prankster trainee.

Res 23

A reservation agent reported selling a seat to a bride-to-be for her wedding dress. The young woman was concerned that the dress would become wrinkled if it were packed, so she purchased a full fare seat for the gown.

Res 24

"Do you fly miniature horses?" (to which I wanted to say . . . no, we fly airplanes. . .).

All of these were sent to us from airline reservations agents who swear they're true . . .

"Do you supply pampers?"

"What is the electric current that is provided at each seat? I need it for my electric breast pump."

"I want a fare price (which is redundant . . a fare IS a price . . I have said a couple of times . . "as opposed to an unfair price?")

Customer: "What time does the plane come in?"
Agent: "Do you know the flight number?"
Customer: "No."
Agent: "Do you have an approximate time it is supposed to arrive?"
Customer: "No."
Agent: "Do you know where it is coming from?"
Customer: "No."
Agent: "What city is it coming into?"
Customer: "Here!"
Agent: "Where is 'here'?"
Customer: "HERE!"....Why are you asking so many questions? Can't you just look out the window and see if it's coming?

Res 25
Then there was a little old lady who was sent to Panama City, Panama instead of Panama City, Florida . . . The things she didn't notice: She was

told she needed to return home and come back to the airport with her passport (which she did). She boarded an Airbus 300, and missed the numerous announcements stating the country to which she was traveling. Her daughter called to make sure the flight was on time, and eventually, everything worked out okay . . She made it to Florida . . via the scenic route.

Res 26
A lady was told that on her flight from Orange County to Oklahoma City that she would have to change in Dallas Fort Worth . . . called Reservations back and asked why she had to change her clothes in Dallas.

Res 27
A customer calling reservations to make some changes was asked by the agent, "Yes ma'am, and what are you holding now?" The reply? "A ham and cheese sandwich."

Res 28
A woman made a reservation for an unaccompanied minor, and let the agent know during the process that she would pay with a credit card. Gathering the information needed for the reservation, the agent asked for and received the child's name. In this case, the child's unusual first name was not easy to identify as being male or

female, so the agent asked, "Is this a 'Master'?" The caller answered, "No, this is a 'Visa'."

Res 29

Another agent swears a caller wanted "drop off service". Seems the would-be passenger wanted to fly to a destination not served by the carrier. When informed of this, and of a major city nearby to which the airline did fly, the passenger (a professional sky-diver) asked if they couldn't just let him jump out of the airplane as it passed over the town he was trying to get to.

Res 30

A reservations agent who spends much of her time handling Latin travel because of her fluency in Spanish reports having extreme difficulty convincing a caller that he could not bring his pet chicken on board the flight in the passenger cabin. She finally got her point across by telling the man, "The only way you're going to bring a chicken on board is to cook him first!"

Res 31

After completing a reservation, the agent went through the recap of all the flight details: departure and arrival time, flight number, the fare and ended by letting the woman know that the equipment for the flight would be an Airbus. The confused caller asked, "I thought I called the airlines. Why are you reserving me a seat on a BUS?"

Res 32

An irate caller demanded to be taken to Miami in the immediate aftermath of Hurricane Andrew. Ignoring the explanation that Miami International Airport was closed to all traffic due to unsafe conditions, she told the dumbfounded agent that she had been planning this vacation for over a year. "If you don't get me there on time", she threatened, "I'll sue!".

One caller informed the agent that he and his wife were frequent fliers on the airline. He wanted to know if, since they always traveled with their dogs and paid the extra fee for them, the animals couldn't get frequent flier numbers too.

Res 34

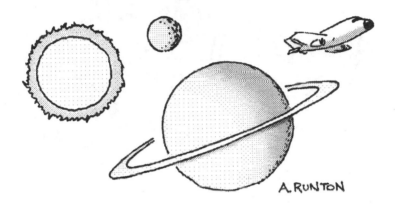

A. RUNTON

There's the lady who called to make plans for her vacation trip to Italy. She insisted that she wanted to fly into, and out of, "Venus".

Res 35

A woman was distressed when the reservations agent explained that she would not be permitted to bring her 5 Himalayan Show Cats on board the flight with her. (There's a limit of one pet per passenger.) She explained that this particular breed of cat has very flat nasal passages and she was concerned that they wouldn't be able to breathe properly in the cargo hold. The agent's suggestion? Amtrak.

Res 36

Many passengers want to carry their pets on board, but the bizarre collection of animal carry-on requests is unbelievable. Pigs, snakes, chickens. . . these are fairly common. One man wanted to take a live turkey with him in the cabin, as he was taking it home for Thanksgiving. Another insisted that his rat was a "pet rat", and when denied permission to bring it on board, threatened to carry it in his pocket.

Res 37

A supervisor reports speaking with an irate lady who was upset about not being able to "make a deal" with the airline. She wanted to cancel her itinerary during the busy holiday travel time and allow the airline to re-sell those prized seats, which she saw as a big favor. In return, she wanted free denied boarding compensation seats in advance. Explaining that while it's true that holiday flights are often overbooked, and frequently free seats are given as compensation for denied boarding, the supervisor denied the passenger's request. "Because passengers book several flights and don't cancel," she explained, "we have no way of knowing which flights will actually be oversold until we see who shows up." Not satisfied, the woman refused to give any information for canceling the flights she didn't intend to use and said in a low, mean-spirited voice, "Two can play at this game!"...and hung up.

Res 38

Reported comments to a reservations agent . . .

"My last flight with you people was 20 minutes late. Please indicate on my ticket that I want an on-time flight."

"You offer special meals? Good, I'll have spaghetti & meatballs."

"When my last flight was delayed, the captain instructed the flight to give everyone a free drink. I was underage at the time, so they wouldn't serve me. Can I get my free drink on this flight? If not, the money will be O.K."

"My Husband's coming into LAX from Seattle. Will that arrive at an international gate?"

"Instead of paying you for this ticket, can I donate an equal amount to the American Cancer Society?"

"It says on my ticket, 'non-refundable'. What does that mean?"

I'm flying tomorrow from Seattle to Moscow, Russia. What else will I need besides my driver's license?"

"Do you people fly to Area Code 304?"

Res 39

When asked for flights to unserved cities, most airlines' reservations agents will refer the caller to a competing airline to help them get where they're going. On one such call, the agent reports telling the passenger that her destination was served by Delta, Continental and American. "Forget it", the caller snarled, "I'm not making that many connections!" . . and hung up!

Res 40

The elderly woman's complaint was being handled by a reservations supervisor, who was more than a little suspicious of the "wait 'till you hear this one" tone in the voice of the agent who'd called her in to help. Nevertheless, she asked the caller to start all over with the reason for her call.

"Well", said the passenger, in a voice that suggested sweet things baking in the kitchen and a kind, uncomplaining disposition, "this was my first time to fly . . . I was going to Peoria to see my granddaughter and her husband, you see, and I was extremely nervous. Everyone had been so kind and patient with me, helping to explain where I was supposed to go, and everything, I was just shocked when the ladies on the airplane were so nasty."

"Do you mean the flight attendants were rude to you?", asked the supervisor. "Well, not just to me," replied the caller, "but to everyone on the airplane. I'm not a prude, and try to be as open minded as the next person, but really, there are limits to what a decent person should say and do in public. This, this was just obscene!"

"Ma'am", said the supervisor, "why don't you just tell me exactly what happened?" "Well, it was just awful", said the caller. "This one girl just walked up and down the aisle, looking right at everyone's private parts! I can tell you, it made a lot of the other passengers look nervous too. I've never been so embarrassed in my life. And what made it worse was that the other lady not only knew what was going on, but even went so far as to announce it over the loudspeaker. She said, "Flight Attendants please prepare all doors for departure and crotch check!!"

Res 41
I once had someone ask if we flew into Long Beach. When I said that we did, he asked if that would be to the Long Beach Airport. "No sir," I answered, "we just sorta fly in real low and flip you out over the bus station".

Res 42
Dealing with a customer angry about ticket prices, the reservationist was not making any headway. The lady was upset and couldn't understand why she was unable to buy a ticket from San Diego to Seattle for $39. When the caller persisted, the agent finally said, "Ma'am, we're the ones with the Eskimo on the tail . . not the dog on the side of the bus!"

Res 43
A new reservations agent got an obscene call from a frequent flyer. He was being lewd and making highly sexually explicit remarks, but he was also making a legitimate reservation, so she stayed on the

line with him. After finishing the call, she came running to a supervisor, explaining what had happened, and asking to leave work immediately to pull herself together. "Oh, I'm really sorry, dear.", said the supervisor, "He upset you THAT badly?" "Well, not exactly", replied the young agent. "You see, I've only been married about a month, and after some of the things he said . . . well, I just know I won't be able to concentrate for the rest of the evening!" The supervisor let her clock out early.

Res 44

A caller once complained to me about the fare we charged from Los Angeles to Portland, Oregon. The ticket price came to $184, round trip, which was a lot lower than the regular, published fare, so I thought it was a pretty good deal. "No, I don't think so", he said. "I'll give you $150. I tried explaining that our ticket prices were fixed and that, while they do go up and down depending on the sales we might have going at a particular time, they are not something I can negotiate. Unimpressed, he replied, "OK, you drive a hard bargain . . . $158!" I kept trying to explain that this really was the fare and that I couldn't do anything to get it any lower. As patiently as I could, I explained that this is already a reduced fare and that, as a result it had some restrictions, and quoted him the regular unrestricted rate. I really thought I was making some headway as he made understanding little "uh-huh", and "I see" comments during my little speech. When I had told him everything I could think of to convince him the fare really was fixed, he paused a bit and said "Fine, here's my final offer . . . $170 . . . take it or leave it."

Res 45

A reservations agent reports receiving a call from a first-time flyer who, when asked if she preferred to have a window or an aisle seat replied, "I'd better take the aisle. I just got my hair done, and wouldn't want to get it messed up."

Res 46

When I was working in Washington, DC, I had an NAACP attorney calling regarding a fare and he told me that he was going to sue me because I said the special fare had blackout dates.

Res 47

A passenger called for information about her upcoming nonstop flight from Phoenix to Newark. She asked the agent how many stops and how long would her layovers be on her nonstop flight.

Res 48

A caller was booking a flight on a domestic carrier and inquired about the type of aircraft being used on the trip. When the agent replied that the equipment would be a Lockheed L-1011, the passenger asked, "Do you know why they call it a 1011?" When the agent admitted she didn't know why, the caller told her, "Because it's late 10 out of 11 times!"

Res 49

A call came into reservations for a flight from Los Angeles to JFK, New York. The schedules were quoted, and the customer asked, "Why does the flight take so long?" The reply was, "the time difference between the west coast and the east coast is 3 hours." The customer asked, "Are you sure it takes that long? I thought planes were jets and go faster nowadays . . ." Again, the reply was, "Sir, you are only on the plane for approximately five and a half hours. The time difference just makes it appear like a longer flight." He asked, "Are you sure you're telling me the non-stop flights? I only want nonstop." The reply from the reservationist again was, "Yes, sir, all these flights I've quoted for you are non-stop." He replied, "I'm going to call another airline to get me there without the time difference."......And disconnected the call.

Res 50

A man called reservations to find out the gate and terminal of a flight that would be arriving later that afternoon. I told him, "Terminal 2E, Gate 22". The passenger then asked, "Is that for first class too?"!!

Res 51

After explaining to a caller that a particular low cost fare required a 7-day advance purchase and a Saturday night stay, he was asked if that meant the passenger had to sleep over. The reply, "No, you're welcome to stay up all night. Sleeping is optional."

29

Res 52

A caller expressed concern about taking "George" with her on board a flight. "Who's George?", asked the agent. Told that "George" was the woman's recently deceased husband, and that she really would appreciate being able to take his ashes aboard, the agent replied that he would make the necessary arrangements, including notifying security and posting a message for the captain. "Never mind", replied the woman. "If it's going to be that much trouble, just throw him on with the luggage."

Res 53

An agent reports that a passenger actually called her to ask for the departure time of the "9:36 flight to Baltimore"!

Res 54

A passenger called to ask the fare from San Francisco to New York. After receiving the information, the caller stated he thought the amount was too expensive and asked the agent to check a

departure from San Jose as an alternative. The reply
. . . "Certainly, sir. Please hold while I transfer you
to International."

Res 55

An agent reports a passenger who booked a flight
and then asked, since the flight was so early, for a
wake-up call. "Sir," was the reply, "we are a full
service airline, but that does have its limits. We
don't provide room service, either."

Res 56

A lady making a reservation for herself and her
mother asked the agent a good many pointed
questions about the seating arrangements. She
absolutely had to sit next to her mother, they
required bulkhead seating, and she wanted as few
passengers around them as possible. Thinking the
last request a bit odd, the agent asked for more
details, and the woman told her that she was
concerned that other passengers would not want to
sit too near them. Curious, the agent asked if there
was a problem. "No", replied the woman, "it's just
that Mom is dead." Then the caller also asked if a
flight attendant could be made available to "keep
Mom from slumping over" if she had to go to the
restroom.

Res 57

A reservations agent reports talking to numerous
passengers who come up with inventive stories to try

to bend the rules. Among the worst are the "seasoned veterans", the Frequent Fliers. They often want to get around the rules for advance purchase, overnight stays or especially, last minute changes to reduced fare tickets. They apparently come up with some tall tales that would make Mark Twain blush. Here's an example:

A woman wanted to use a non-refundable, reduced fare ticket for a flight she had failed to take over two months before. She claimed that when she originally called to request a change, an airline agent told her that service to her destination was seasonal, and she'd just have to stay in New York until service to that city resumed. As a result, this woman said she lost her job, her boyfriend, and perhaps her furniture, as it was moved out of her apartment when she was not at home to pay the rent. She also asked for compensation for her two dogs' vaccinations, claiming that her forced stay had caused their tags to expire.

After hearing stories like these, the agent reports that the excuses were really starting to get her. Instead of answering one call with the standard greeting, she Freudian slipped, "Frequent *Liar* Desk, may I help you?"

Res 58
A man called to book a flight and, after settling the details of time, date, and flight number, the

agent asked him for his personal information to complete the reservation. "I'll need your name, please, last name first."

"First" was the reply.
"No, sir", said the agent, "I need your last name."
"First", he said again.

The agent became increasingly irritated as this exchange continued, before finally realizing that the man was *indeed* giving her his last name. He was Mr. First. With this settled, she asked for his first name, and was confused when the passenger replied, "Why?"

"Because I need to have your full name to complete this reservation!", the agent said, again becoming irritated.

"Why?", repeated the passenger.
"Sir, if you want to complete this reservation, I'll need your first name!"
"Why, why, why!" shouted the frustrated Mr. First. "My name is Wai First!"

Res 59

Anyone who answers the phone for a living can expect a fair share of crank calls. You can only imagine how many obscene calls the airlines get, but this gets some sort of prize for unusual fetishes . . .

A major airline reservations agent reports a caller whose calls always started out with the usual inquires about fares, discounts, restrictions, and the like. The questions would get more and more detailed, involving everything from special meals to senior discounts. Finally, after 30 minutes or so of everything under the sun, the caller would agree to book the flight and prepare to read the agent a credit card number. Exactly in the middle of the card number, the caller would pause and shout, "Oh! Oh! There's a BUG on my leg!" He'd scream, then there would be a loud stomping noise, after which the man would say, "I've just killed a bug with my bare feet. It's disgusting. It's all over my foot." He'd then ask the agent how she (the caller only pulled this routine on female agents) felt about mashed cockroach, laugh hysterically and hang up.

The agent reports this caller calling repeatedly, sometimes several times a night. No wonder it takes so long to get an agent on the phone.

The Airport

Airport 1

A gate agent reports receiving a reprimand for these "heroics" . . .

After closing out the last flight, an agent was approached by a hassled businessman, who asked for the correct gate information for his flight. Checking the computer, the agent gave him the gate number, which was about as far away as possible without leaving the airport. The man sprinted off in the proper direction.

About ten minutes later, the agent was walking down the concourse when he encountered the same man, running in the opposite direction. On inquiry, he learned that the man had gone to the assigned gate, but that no one was there . . . no agents, no passengers, no airplane. He was now trying to run back up front to the information counter, as all the monitors in sight showed the same wrong gate he'd already been given.

Quickly grabbing his two-way radio, the agent called dispatch and learned that the flight was indeed at another gate, all the way on the other end of the terminal, and boarding NOW. Seeing a tug outside on the ramp, the agent asked the passenger if he was game for a wild ride. When the man replied he was, he found himself outside, in the rain, driving across the ramp at break neck speed on a topless aircraft tug.

The passenger, a little soggy and windblown, made his flight. The agent got a good chewing from his boss, appreciative remarks from his coworkers and forever after, the nickname, "Tug".

Airport 2

Last night I was sitting at the gate, more than ready to work the final flight of the long day, Flight 2398 to Las Vegas. As happens more often than I like, it was running late. I had just finished changing the sign behind me to read,

"FLIGHT 2398 - LAS VEGAS - DELAYED TO 12:25"

A passenger walked up to me and, despite the sign behind me in bright red letters, asked me, "What happened to the 11:59 flight to Las Vegas??" I didn't want to laugh in her face, but I looked at her and I looked at the sign and said, "It's right here, see: DELAYED TO 12:25." She said, "Oh, but what about the 11:59 flight?"

Airport 3

A passenger boarded a flight from Columbus, Ohio, to Phoenix, Arizona, and took his seat in the first class cabin. Since the first class passengers had boarded first, there was at least 20 minutes left before departure. Like a lot of road warriors, the man immediately took advantage of the extra few minutes of peace and quiet by falling asleep. He was soon snoring so loudly that he had the attention of many of the passengers and crew within earshot. As he slept, all the remaining passengers had boarded and the flight was just moments away from backing away from the gate. Suddenly, the sleeper jolted awake, looked about in obvious confusion, snatched his suitcase from the overhead and rushed off the aircraft past a startled flight attendant. In the process, the man nearly bowled over the gate agent walking down the jetway with the final paperwork for the flight.

The gate agent and pursuing flight attendant managed to convince the confused flyer that he was still in Columbus and returned him to his seat. As he re-stowed his luggage, the red-faced man announced to the other amused first class passengers, "That was the shortest flight to Phoenix I've ever had!"

Airport 4
An airline employee, who happened to have the last name of Gay, got on a plane recently using one of his company's "Free Flight" programs. However, when Mr Gay tried to take his seat, he found it being occupied by a paying passenger. So, not to make a fuss, he simply chose another seat.

Unknown to Mr. Gay, another company flight at the airport experienced mechanical problems. The passengers of this other flight were being rerouted to various airplanes. A few were put on Mr. Gay's flight and anyone who was holding a "free" ticket was being "bumped".

Airline officials, armed with a list of these "freebie" passengers, boarded the plane to remove the free ticket holders. Of course, our Mr. Gay was not sitting in his assigned seat as you may remember. So when the gate agent approached the seat where Mr. Gay was supposed to be sitting, she asked a startled customer, "Are you Gay?". The man shyly nodded that he was, at which point she told him, "Then you have to get off the plane.".

Our Mr. Gay, overhearing what the gate agent had said, tried to clear up the situation, "You've got the wrong man, I'm Gay!". This caused an angry third passenger to yell, "Hell, I'm gay, too!" They can't kick us all off!"

Confusion reigned as more and more passengers began yelling that the airline had no right to remove gays from their flights. To avoid causing any more trouble, all "gays" were allowed to remain on the flight.

Airport 5
A young copilot for a major carrier takes his physical fitness seriously, and carries running shoes and attire with him on all his trips, using a backpack to keep his hands free for other carry-on items.

Recently he reported walking through a terminal and noticing that many of the passengers were grinning at him as he walked through the concourse. Assuming they must recognize him from other flights, he smiled and nodded at them as he made his way to his departure gate.

Feeling really important, he boarded his flight, stowed his luggage and found the sign someone had pinned to the backpack: "PARACHUTE".

Airport 6
Overheard in the baggage check-in line:

The female ticket agent is checking the bags for an older man, including a heavy set of golf clubs which he is struggling to get up on the recessed baggage area for tagging. "Sir", she exclaimed, "your zipper is open and your balls are falling on the floor!"

Airport 7
A passenger checked in for his flight to Detroit. When the agent asked if he had luggage to check , the man replied, "Yes, two bags. Send this on to Los Angeles, and the small brown one goes to Dallas." "Sir, I'm sorry, but we are not permitted to send your bags to anyplace but your destination, so we can't send these bags to Los Angeles and Dallas."

"Why not?", asked the traveler, "That's what you did last week!"

Airport 8

A passenger checked in for his flight to Phoenix from Nashville with a change of planes in St. Louis. He was carrying two rather large pieces of luggage, which the agent doubted could fit in the overhead. The agent asked the man about checking the bags, and was told in no uncertain terms, "I NEVER check my luggage. The orangutans you people use for ground handlers could tear up an anvil!" The passenger was adamant that his luggage would fit on the cabin, and though the flight was very full and the passenger was just barely going to make it to the gate on time, he issued the ticket and sent the man on his way. When the passenger arrived at the aircraft, everyone was on board and, indeed, there was no space for the large bags. He walked on, dropped his overstuffed garment bags at the feet of a rather petite flight attendant and said, in a very annoyed voice, "Do something with these!". He then took his seat in first class. After the flight took off, the flight attendant gave the him two check stubs. The passenger looked confused and asked, "What's this?". The attendant said, "You told me to do something with your bags, so I did. I checked them!"

Airport 9

A passenger reports standing in line to check in for a flight from London to Boston behind the

41

original "Ugly American". This guy made frequent, loud, and obscene comments about the service and the amount of time he was being forced to wait. Others in line were relieved when his turn finally came, just so they wouldn't have to listen to him any more.

The female agent who was unlucky enough to draw this character became his next target. He unloaded on her for having to wait, the poor seat assignment, the cost of the ticket, and everything except the weather. During all this abuse, the agent remained cheerful, pleasant, and smiling. She never allowed any of the man's rude comments to alter her sweet demeanor. When the man finally stomped off, still fuming, the next passenger commented on how sweetly she'd handled a difficult passenger.

The agent responded with her bright smile and said, "That's OK. He's going to Boston, but his luggage is going to Bangladesh!"

Airport 10
A would-be passenger, seeing the cancellation of the last flight to Omaha on the monitor, waits in line to ask the agent,"I see that the Omaha flight has been cancelled. When will it be departing?" The answer, "Tomorrow."

Airport 11
While talking to a customer service agent in the

terminal at Washington's Dulles Airport, a ticketed passenger asked for directionss to the closest place he could smoke. The reply was, "Philadelphia".

Airport 12

Pet peeve from a gate agent: I hate it when I walk out into the terminal in uniform and people walk up to me as if I had a sign over my head saying "information". They ask me which gate their flight will be leaving from, or if they are waiting for someone, they ask which gate is that flight coming in at. I always answer, "You might want to ask the information desk for more details on that flight". What I'd really like to do is put my hands on my temple like Johnny Carson's "Great Carnac" and, psychically produce the answer, "Oh, Ok, it's coming to me now. It looks like it's going to be gate D5!"

Airport 13

I was working the gate at my commuter airline for a flight from St. Louis to Sioux City. The flight was delayed approximately 60 minutes (on a 1-1/2 hour flight) and one lady came up and asked me, "Since my flight to Sioux City is delayed, does that mean I'll get there late?" I told her, "Yes, the aircraft will arrive late." She then asked me, "Well, can't the pilots make it go faster?"

Airport 14

There's the lady who called the check-in counter

concerned because she was going to miss her flight..
.. it was leaving in 10 minutes and the plane hadn't
come to pick her up yet.

Airport 15

A last minute passenger rushes onto a flight which
was ready to push back. Obviously following
instruction from the gate agent, he breathlessly asks
the flight attendants, "Which seats are the vacant
ones?" The attendants are laughing too hard to
attempt to reply.

Airport 16
During the holiday season, many passengers were frustrated due to heavy fog which was delaying and cancelling flights into and out of Seattle. One caller demanded that the agent tell her when the fog was going to lift. When the agent (who happened to be in an office in Denver) told the passenger she didn't know, the exasperated woman asked, "Well, it *will* be gone by tomorrow morning, won't it?"

Airport 17
Huffing, sweating, and out of breath, a Memphis passenger arrived at the gate for the 8 am flight to Atlanta at 8:10. "Am I late?" he gasped to the gate agent.

Without hesitation, she replied coolly, "No, sir, you're just about 2 hours early for the 10:00 flight.

Airport 18
A woman checking in for a flight from Atlanta to Frankfurt, Germany, was told at the check-in counter that she had more than the allowable two pieces of checked baggage. Playing all her trump cards (a super-frequent flyer status with the carrier, a scathing tongue, and a nasty disposition) she at length browbeat the agent into allowing her to take the extra bags at no charge.

After her stay, the lady had already determined that she would again pay no extra to return home with her excess bags, but her technique made absolutely no impression on the German agent. If she wanted to take extra bags, she'd pay extra . . . period.

But in addition to being persuasive, she considered herself very clever and thought of a way around the system. After checking all that was allowed with her carrier, she proceeded to take the rest of her bags to the counter of another carrier with a flight departing to Atlanta at about the same time. She bought a full-fare ticket on that flight and checked her luggage, intending to claim the bags in Atlanta and then apply for a full refund on the unused ticked.

The lady had everything figured out. Everything, that is, but the very strict European security measures. Passengers and checked bags are matched very carefully over there to lessen the chance of terrorism.

So when no passenger checked in on the flight who matched the extra bags, they were immediately taken to a bomb disposal area and burned.

As a post script to the story, you will probably not be surprised to hear that the passenger called the *original* carrier after she learned of the fate of her bags, demanding full compensation for the value of her goods.

A gate agent related this story . . . Working a flight to Las vegas, the agent went on board to take a final empty seat count and noticed a woman with a toy French Poodle, neatly harnessed and seat belted in the seat next to her. Approaching the passenger, she explained that the dog couldn't sit in the seat, but would have to travel in the under seat carrier at the woman's feet. The passenger became very upset, announcing that she had paid extra for the dog to travel with her, and insisting on using the extra seat.

The agent tried to explain that the extra payment did not entitle the dog to a seat of its own, but the lady became more and more upset, finally getting up, gathering up her dog and belongings and storming off to the front of the airplane. Quickly completing her seat count, the agent walked toward the exit, trying to decide how to deal with the unreasonable passenger. Turning the corner to the cabin door, she found the lady, all strapped into a flight attendant's jump seat, arms folded and with a determined look on her face. The dog? Strapped into the other flight attendant's jump seat, all ready to go.

Airport 20
A gate agent in Phoenix made the final call for Flight 203 to Pittsburgh, announcing, "This will be your final call for Flight 302 . . . (pause) . . . Flight 203 to Pittsburgh." And then not realizing that she had not released the microphone key, "Oh, s..t!" Several of the passengers approached the embarrassed agent and asked, "Is it time to get on "Old Oh S..t"?".

Airport 21
On board in 1st class, a Royal Princess from a third world country was acting really "snooty" and "rude"

to a female flight attendant during boarding. It came time to prepare the cabin for taxi and the flight attendant asked the "Princess" to take a seat and fasten her seatbelt. She responded that in her country she didn't have to abide by rules meant for "commoners". The attendant was getting a little intimidated by the passenger and asked again, nicely, informing her that in our country this is a requirement of the law. The Princess yelled back at the attendant, "I'm known as a Princess where I'm from and I don't have to!"

Just then a gay male flight attendant was walking by and noticed what was going on. He said to the Princess, "Well, where I'm from I'm known as a "Queen". I outrank you, so sit down right now and fasten your seatbelt."

Airport 22
An exhibitionist was preparing to board a flight to Chicago. As he approached the open door of the plane at the end of the jetway, a very attractive flight attendant was collecting boarding passes. As she reached toward him for his boarding pass, he opened his raincoat and exposed himself.

"I'm sorry, sir", she said politely, "but you have to show your ticket here, not your stub."

Airport 23
A passenger was going through security and

something in one of his bags aroused suspicion in the x-ray tech doing the scanning. The bag was pulled aside and the passenger was asked by a guard if it would be okay for her to look inside.

The passenger, looking rather embarrassed, replied that he'd really rather not have her look in there, since the bag contained several sex toys of an obviously personal nature. Stuttering and stammering, the passenger retrieved all of his luggage and then went to the airline's check-in counter where he apparently had decided to check the bags, rather than carry them on, thus avoiding the embarrassing exposure of his personal toys.

The security guard remained suspicious and called a supervisor to pass on what had happened. The supervisor immediately called airport police, who detained the passenger and his luggage. Upon inspection, the "toys" in the bag turned out to be 8 ounces of cocaine.

Airport 24
A male passenger sprinted up to the gate, panting heavily, only to see that the jetway door was closed and the airplane was being pushed back from the gate. Rushing to the ticket counter, the man cornered a female agent and shouted, "What are you people doing??? This flight was scheduled to depart at 8:05, and according to my watch, it's only 8:04!!!"

"I'm sorry, sir," replied the agent, "but when I closed the flight, you weren't here, so I had to use my watch."

Airport 25

Friday evening at Chicago's O'Hare Airport, and the 9:00 flight to New York has just cancelled. Nearly one hundred angry, frustrated, and anxious would-be passengers are lined up for what seems like half the length of the concourse. At the head of this line is just one gate agent, bravely smiling as she tries to help customers arrange alternate bookings or find hotel accommodations. Some seem more interested in having someone to vent their frustration at than in anything else, but she gamely tries to help each one, filing away for future consideration some of the suggestions about what she can do with their useless tickets and "her" broken airplanes.

In the midst of this turmoil, an extremely well-dressed man storms up to the counter and slams his expensive briefcase down in front of the startled agent. In a loud voice, he demands to be placed on the next flight to New York . . . immediately!

She patiently explains to the passenger, "Sir, if you'll look behind you, you'll notice there are quite a few people in exactly your same situation. I'm extremely sorry that we've had this delay, and I'm trying to help all of these passengers as quickly as possible. If you'll just take a place in line, I'll do everything possible to help you, too."

Hoping that her calm tone and professional manner have had the desired effect, she starts to turn back to the person she'd been helping when the impatient passenger exclaims in a voice loud enough to be heard by everyone in the area. "Do you *know* who I am!!????" Without the slightest hesitation, the gate agent picks up the microphone at the podium and announces over the gate's loudspeaker, "Ladies and gentlemen in the area of Gate 17, there is a passenger at the front who does not know who he is. If there's anyone in the area who can help identify this passenger, please come to the counter."

Red-faced, angry and embarrassed, the impatient passenger snatches his briefcase off the counter and snarls, "Screw you, lady."

"Sir", she replies evenly, "you'll have to stand in line for that, too."

Airport 26
During the "rush hour" at Houston's Hobby Airport, a flight was delayed due to a mechanical problem. Since they needed the gate for another flight, the aircraft was backed away from the gate while the maintenance crew worked on it.

The passengers were then told the new gate number, which was some distance away. Everyone moved to the new gate, only to find that a third gate had been designated. After some further shuffling, everyone got on board and as they were settling in, the flight attendant made the usual announcement:

"We apologize for the inconvenience of this last-minute gate change. This flight is going to Washington, D.C. If your destination is not Washington, D.C., then you should de-plane at this time.

A very confused-looking and red-faced pilot emerged from the cockpit, carrying his bags. "Sorry," he said, "wrong plane."

Airport 27
Remember the old song, ,"The M.T.A.", about the passenger on the Boston subway who never could get off? "He may ride forever, beneath the streets of Boston. He's the man who'll never return . . . " There's a report from a gate agent who followed the adventure of one poor soul who must have felt that way.

This passenger started in Atlanta, headed to Philadelphia, but somehow boarded the wrong plane and wound up in Indianapolis. Due to his arrival time, there were no more flights to Philly that evening, so the passenger was provided accommodations and dinner by the airline and scheduled for a morning flight on to Philadelphia.

The agent working his departure out of Atlanta was notified of the error, via teletype, and pulled up the passenger's itinerary on the computer to see how he made out. Turns out the confused fella came to the airport the next morning and mistakenly got on a flight to Minneapolis. We're not sure if he ever got where he meant to go.

Airport 28
On a flight from Miami to Orlando, I had made a PA that all bags should be stowed beneath the seat or in the overhead bin (OHB) prior to taxi. I made a visual check of the cabin. One man had his bags out. I asked him to stow the bags. I needed to ask him twice. Finally, I asked him if he would like me to place the bags under the seat or in the OHB, as we wanted to get going. The man replied to me, "Oh, have you been talking to me all that time? I'm a gold level frequent flyer, you know". Guess he must have been unconscious, drunk, or asleep while he flew all those miles required for gold frequent flyer status.

Airport 29
A flight attendant reports checking in passengers at the aircraft's main door. As a man boarded, he confidently said, "They've already checked my boarding card at the gate." The attendant informed him that she really needed to double-check it, so

impatiently, the man handed the card over.

"It's a good thing I checked, sir", she said, "because this card says you're going to Syracuse."

"Correct-a-mundo", he said smugly. "I'm going to Syracuse. This is the flight to Syracuse. Now, may I please sit down?"

"Sir", the attendant replied, "this is *not* the flight to Syracuse. This aircraft is going to Green Bay."

"Impossible!", insisted the passenger. "The gate board says this is the flight to Syracuse. Don't you people even keep track of where you're going?"

The flight attendant tried to explain that the board might be for a later flight to Syracuse leaving from this gate, but that *this* flight was definitely going to Green Bay. He continued to argue with her, insisting that this was the flight to Syracuse, until she tired of trying to convince him. Picking up the airplane's P.A. mike, she announced, "Will all those passengers going to Syracuse please raise their hand?" Naturally, no one responded. She glanced at the stubborn passenger and announced, "Will all those passengers going to Green Bay, please raise their hand?" Since this was a non-stop flight, everyone responded.

Smiling sweetly, the attendant returned the

passenger's boarding card. He snatched it from her grasp and, though obviously wrong, still insisted on the last word. As he stomped back up the ramp to find the real flight to Syracuse, he muttered over his shoulder, "First damned airplane I ever saw going someplace on a vote. You probably stuffed the ballot box!"

Airport 30

My boss was working on the ramp for a major airline when one of the ramp guys came over and alerted him to a problem. He investigated and found an animal container with a dead dog inside. They both determined that the dog must have got put into the wrong cargo area of the plane and died for lack of oxygen and heat. The ramp person stated that he was looking for a dog at the pound near the airport the previous day and saw a dog EXACTLY like this one. They agreed to exchange the dogs hoping to satisfy the owner and, in some way, make up for the loss of the animal. After quickly securing the replacement and putting it in the kennel, they went up to the baggage claim to see what was going to happen. Well, when the dog came down the baggage belt, it was just wagging its tail intensely. A woman standing nearby fainted. The two guys helped her come to, asked her if she was OK, and why she had such a reaction. She replied that she was transporting her dog back to her home town where it was to be buried and, to her shock, found a resurrected dog right in front of her!

Airport 31

Shortly after takeoff, a very nervous passenger called the flight attendant over to report strange noise. He'd gotten up to retrieve something out of the overhead, and heard an unusual humming noise coming from one of the bags. The attendant, hearing the sound, immediately went to the cockpit to report the suspicious luggage.

The captain, fearing there might be some terrorist device on board that had slipped through security, made a P.A. announcement requesting the owner of the bag to identify himself. After receiving no response, the captain immediately contacted Air Traffic Control, requested, and received clearance to return for an immediate landing.

The aircraft landed safely, much to the relief of the concerned passengers and crew. Security personnel boarded the plane immediately when it reached the gate and gingerly removed the suspect luggage from the overhead bin. At this point the bag was identified by a red-faced woman who had slept through all the excitement. Under the careful scrutiny of the security folks, she reached into the bag and turned off her vibrator.

Airport 32

With her 4 year old daughter in tow, an extremely attractive passenger approached the baggage claim counter to file a claim for a missing

58

bag. She gave the agent her name and address, a brief description of the suitcase and then was asked for information about the contents, in case that became necessary for identification.

She was giving the agent a list of some of the items in her luggage when her daughter began tugging on her pant leg. "Mommy", shouted the child, "don't forget to tell him about your vibrator!"

To break the silence which fell among the passengers and agents at the counter, the agent told the red-faced woman, "Ma'am, I think we have quite enough information to locate your bag."

Airport 33

A commuter pilot reports flying fairly often with female pilots on the crew. Women are indeed seen more frequently in the cockpit as they make inroads into the formerly all-male career. Most passengers have become so accustomed to seeing female pilots that it rarely merits notice, let alone comment. But there are always those who seem to live with one foot planted firmly in the 19th Century . . .

One such passenger approached this pilot after a recent rip on which the other pilot happened to be female. "Don't worry, son," said the elderly gentleman with a lascivious wink, "I won't tell anyone that you let the *Stewardess* sit up front."

A.RUNTON

Passengers impatiently waiting at the gate to board a flight already considerably "behind schedule" were given this creative explanation over the P.A.:

"Ladies and gentlemen, we apologize for this delay. The machine that normally rips the handles off your luggage is broken, so we're having to do it by hand. We should be finished and have you on your way shortly."

Airport 35

An elderly woman nervously waited in the check-in line at Miami International for her first ever airline flight. After going through the usual scrutiny of identification and baggage check, she was directed toward the end of the counter and another line. She was told by the agent that she could "pick up her seat" there. "Oh my," said the old lady timidly, "I haven't felt very well lately. I hope I won't have to carry it too far."

Airport 36

A passenger checking in at Chicago's O'Hare Airport during a typical Midwest snowstorm was told by the agent that his flight had been delayed for two hours due to the weather. The man became furious, exclaiming, "Can't any of you airlines run on time?". He continued to rant and rave at the female ticket agent, liberally spicing his commentary on airline inefficiency with expletives. Trying to be soothing and offering her apologies, the agent was getting nowhere with the passenger. At this point, a rather large man, standing in line behind the irate passenger tapped him on the shoulder.

"Listen, Pal", said the second passenger, "how long did it take you to get to the airport this morning?"

The first passenger whirled around and found himself looking directly at the knot in the much larger man's tie. "Why, about two hours", was the considerably restrained reply.

"Well, it seems to me that it must be harder to fly in this snowstorm than to drive in it, so why don't you back off?"

The agent completed the check in for the much subdued passenger and thanked the large man for his help. After completing her shift, the weary gal made her usual 30 minute drive home. . . in just under 3 hours.

Airport 37

A counter supervisor for an airline operating out of Newark was asked to take a call from an irate customer. It seemed the woman was upset because the agent she'd been talking to had refused to page an arriving passenger. Using her most professional, soothing voice, the supervisor asked the caller to explain her problem.

"It's very simple," stated the woman, "all I want is for you people to page Eric for me."

"I certainly see no problem with that. What's Eric's last name?"

"I don't know," answered the caller.

"I see," replied the supervisor, already suspecting that she didn't really. "Well, can you tell me what flight Eric was supposed to arrive on?" Naturally, the woman had no clue about the flight number. Hoping for anything that might help narrow the field, the supervisor then asked, "Could you tell me what city Eric is coming in from?" Again the caller didn't have that trivial piece of information. "Ma'am, it's going to be very difficult for me to help you if we don't know more about this passenger. There are probably dozens of people in the Newark Airport right now whose first name is Eric. Can you at least confirm for me that Eric arrived on our airline?"

"I don't know what airline he arrived on!", shouted the caller. "I don't know why you people won't hlep me. All I'm trying to do is to let him know that I can't be there to pick him up! No wonder everyone says flying is such a hassle!" . . . and hung up.

Flt 1

A businessman was seated next to a nursing mother who was feeding her baby as the aircraft descended. Concerned that the man might be embarrassed by her nursing, she explained that she was feeding the baby at that time to help him unblock his little ears.

The man lowered his glasses onto his nose and with a discreet glance at the baby said, "And to think, I always just chew gum."

Flt 2

A mother and her seven year old son were flying on a major carrier from Kansas City to Chicago. The boy, who had been lost in thought looking out the window, turned to his mother and asked, "If big dogs have baby dogs, and big cats have baby cats, why don't big airplanes have baby planes?" The mother couldn't think of an answer that didn't involve a discussion she wasn't prepared for, so she dodged by telling the boy to ask the flight attendant.

When the boy repeated his question to the first passing attendant, she asked him if his mother had told him to ask her that question. He replied that she had. The attendant thought a moment and said, "Tell your mommy that this airline always pulls out on time."

We've all heard the invitation countless times: "If there's anything we can do to make your flight more comfortable, just let us know." Apparently a man on a flight from New York to Tucson took the flight attendants at their word.

Shortly after takeoff, the passenger switched to an

aisle seat and stripped to his jockey shorts. He sat for the duration of the flight to the intermediate stop, Cincinnati, in this state of undress, despite protests from the crew. The airplane was met in Cincinnati by police and airline personnel who confiscated his ticket, cancelled his reservations and escorted him from the terminal.

The man explained his actions, saying that he really thought they wanted him to be comfortable; anyway, they were *long* jockey shorts; and besides, he came from a liberal family. Airline officials were unimpressed with these excuses.

After spending the night in Cincinnati at his own expense, the passenger called the airline back to beg for reinstatement of his ticket, claiming sleep deprivation as the culprit for his behavior. After extracting solemn promises from the man, the carrier allowed him to continue to Tucson. The passenger completed the trip with his pants on.

Flt 4

This from a flight attendant . . . I was working a crowded flight to Albuquerque, and stayed extremely busy with the boarding process. When I was finally able to take my jump seat for departure, I noticed a little old lady trying to get my attention. We were on the runway, and as we started takeoff roll, the woman started to leave her seat. I quickly unbuckled and told her to stay in her seat. It became apparent that she spoke no English, but I believed she was trying to tell me she needed to use the rest room. I signalled to her that she would have to wait, and that I'd be back to get her when it was safe to get up.

When the seatbelt sign went out, I got the lady and escorted her to the lavatory, helped her in and closed the door. She immediately opened the door and came out. As I quickly became busy with other duties, I paid no further attention to the little lady until we arrived and I noticed her in an animated conversation with the gate agent. Walking up to them, I asked if there was a problem. The agent told me that the woman had intended to go to Philadelphia and, after realizing that she was on the wrong plane, tried to tell several flight attendants, but all they did was take her to the bathroom.

Flt 5

It's tough on smokers in the U.S. these days. Perhaps even more so if the smoker is from out of town. So it was on April 10 when an Italian tried to light up in the lavatory of a Milan-to-Newark flight. The crew decided to divert to Bangor, Maine, where the man was deplaned and arrested. He pleaded guilty to an assault charge and received a seven-day sentence in the local hoosegow, plus a $1,000 fine. The punch line: The Bangor jail had a no-smoking policy.

Flt 6

Exchange between departing aircraft and air traffic control tower . . .

Tower: Eastern 702, cleared for takeoff, contact Departure on 124.7."

Eastern 702: "Tower, Eastern 702 switching to Departure . . . by the way, as we lifted off, we saw some kind of dead animal on the far end of the runway."

Tower: "Eastern 635, cleared for takeoff, contact Departure on 124.7 . . . did you copy the report about the dead animal?"

Eastern 635: "Eastern 635, yes, we copied the report and we've already notified our caterers."

Flt 7

A flight attendant recalled a trip to Las Vegas when an older man approached her with an embarrassing question. He explained that his wife had been in the lavatory and somehow had lost her false teeth in the toilet. He wondered if it were possible for him to try to fish them out.

Not being sure of the mechanics, the attendant asked the captain if it was dangerous for the man to make the attempt. The captain stopped laughing long enough to let her know that as unsanitary as it might be, it was not hazardous to get into the holding tank.

She relayed the message, gave the gentleman a

garbage bag and wished him luck. He emerged about 20 minutes later with a dripping bag and a smile, saying he had found the missing choppers. He gave the bag to the attendant who placed it inside a clean bag and stored it until arrival.

After all this trouble, she reports that the couple deplaned without the teeth. The story ended with our intrepid attendant chasing the couple through the concourse, shouting for them to stop and get their teeth.

Flt 8

My girlfriend and I were flying first class to Disney World, and the flight attendant brought us our meal which was half frozen. When I brought this to his attention he apologized and said he didn't know how to cook.

Flt 9

Three hours into the flight out of LAX, an obviously worried man stopped a passing flight attendant and asked, "It seems like we've been flying a long time. When do we arrive in Oakland?" "Oakland?", she replied, "Sir, you're on a flight to Auckland, New Zealand!"

Flt 10

An Indian passenger, traveling on a jumbo transatlantic flight rang his attendant call button repeatedly with no results. Becoming more and more impatient, he finally left his seat to complain to the in-flight service coordinator. When asked the nature of his problem, he explained, "I keep fingering her and fingering her, but she no come!"

Flt 11
On an overnight flight from Japan to L.A., a flight attendant made the announcement that the lights in the cabin would be turned off to allow passengers to sleep. A Japanese couple promptly got up and went back to the lavatory. They returned to their seats dressed in pajamas. The man then began helping his wife boost herself up into the overhead luggage compartment, apparently thinking that this was a "sleeping car" . . .

Flt 12
A passenger receiving his complementary meal on a cross country flight reportedly asked the flight attendant if he could pay for that with food stamps.

Flt 13
A flight attendant recalls seeing an elderly female passenger with the little in-flight headset earpieces shoved firmly up her nose. Cautiously, she approached the woman and asked if she needed any help. The passenger replied, "No, thanks. I just needed a little oxygen."

Flt 14

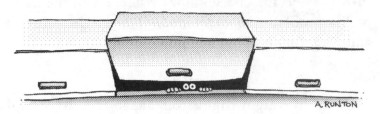

A flight attendant, making her final rounds before takeoff asked a young couple with a baby and a rather large stroller to "stow that" in the luggage bin, pointing to the stroller. Checking again on her way back forward, she noticed no stroller . . . and no baby. Stopping to ask the obvious question, she discovered the stroller . . . and the baby . . . neatly stowed in the overhead.

Flt 15

Something to think about while you're ignoring the next pre-flight emergnecy briefing . . .

A veteran flight attendant tells us of observing passengers, even those sitting in the emergency exit rows, that come to the back of the airplane to use the lavatory and ask, "how do you open the lav door?" She simply replies, "turn the handle." What concerns her is that these same people are sitting next to the exit, and they're supposed to help open the exit in case of an emergency. How could they do that when they can't even figure out how to open the LAVATORY door?!!!

Flt 16

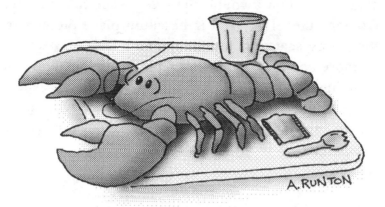

While in Boston, flight attendants can take advantage of buying live lobsters freshly packaged in ice to take home. So a group of flight attendants purchased their lobsters and brought them on board their Boston-L.A. flight. These flight attendants thought it would be fun to share their "purchases" with the first class passengers.

When the time came for the in-flight meal service, flight attendants took the lobsters out of their containers, placed them on an airline tray with salad, roll and desert, and "pretended" to offer this to the passengers as their meal choice of the day. Mind you, the lobsters were alive and moving on the tray. One passenger exclaimed, "Now that's the freshest airline meal I've ever seen!"

Flt 17

On a flight, I asked a young man to please stow

73

his box either under the seat or in the overhead. He said that that would be disrespectful to his Grandmother. He asked if he could place the box in the empty seat next to him because Grandma would be more comfortable. I was a bit suspicious until he explained that the box continued Grandma's ashes. She had never taken a flight--this was her first time in an airplane. With the captain's permission, Grandma "sat" in the window seat.

Flt 18
Believe it or not, a flight attendant won an employee contest with this true story.

On a short domestic flight, the kind with a full house and the attendants running up and down the aisle like a Western Union messenger with his shoes on fire, trying to serve everyone at least a drink and a half-stale bag of peanuts, a lady passenger stopped the attendant. With a conspiratorial glance at her young son sitting beside her, she whispered, "It's my son's birthday. If you have an extra cake and some candles on board, I'd really like to surprise him."

Flt 19
This story happened on board a flight from Miami to Boston during a recent hurricane. The captain did his best to skirt the edge of the storm, but it was a pretty rough ride just the same - - rough enough that the flight attendants were ordered to strap themselves into their seats for about half an hour,

and many of the passengers were putting the little plastic-lined bags in their seat pockets to good use. When the turbulence finally abated, the flight attendants unbuckled themselves and the captain's voice came over the intercom. "Well, folks, that was quite some ride, wasn't it? But we came through it fine, just the way we always do, and I'm happy to report that it looks like the remainder of our trip should be much calmer. On behalf of myself and today's flight crew, I'd like to thank you very much for your calmness and co-operation, and extend our best wishes for a pleasant stay in Boston."

After a short pause and several clicks . . .

"Geez - whadda bitchin' ride! Boy--I sure could use a good strong cup of coffee and a b... j.. right about now." As a stricken flight attendant dashed up the aisle to the cockpit to inform the captain that his intercom was still on, one of the passengers called after her ,"Don't forget the coffee!"

Flt 20
We blew out an engine on a 757 right after takeoff from Detroit going to Orlando. The captain finally came over the P.A. and told the passengers the usual "don't worry this plane flies well on just one engine. etc., etc." The crew performed professionally, getting the now single-engine airplane back to the runway at Detroit. To everyone's relief, we landed safely. After we got back to the terminal, the gate

75

agent came on board to tell the passengers that the flight was going to be cancelled and to come to the ticket counter for alternate arrangements. One lady asked loudly, "Well if it flies just as well on one engine as two, like the pilot said, why didn't we just keep on going to Orlando?"

Flt 21

On the way to Palm Beach one night, a woman rang the call button from about row 20 on a DC9. When the flight attendant went back, the passenger complained that it was too noisy back there. The attendant explained that the engines were indeed loud in this part of the cabin, and apologized. The flight was very full, ruling out the option of changing seats, so there was nothing she could do. The passenger then asked, very seriously, "Can't they shut them off for a while?"

Flt 22

On board a flight from San Francisco to Honolulu, a passenger stopped a flight attendant to ask if this was going to be a non-stop flight. The answer? "I sure hope so!"

Flt 23

As a flight attendant based in Orlando, I am used to planes full of rowdy kids headed for Disney World. One flight from Rhode Island to Orlando was especially nerve-racking, thanks to two young brothers who were very poorly behaved. They were constantly running up and down the aisles and getting into things in the galley. After finally completing the service, I was in the rear of the plane next to the door attempting a few moments of rest when the youngest brother came over and peered out the window. "Wow", he said, noting that we were well above the clouds, "are we in Heaven?" "No", I replied, "I'm pretty positive this is NOT Heaven!"

Flt 24

On a flight from New York to L.A., one of the first class passengers had more than a little too much to drink. As the young and very attractive flight attendant was pouring coffee for the passenger directly across the aisle, he impulsively reached over and patted her behind.

Furious, the woman whirled around and put her fist right under the man's nose. "Don't you *ever* touch me again", she hissed.

It was not too long after this incident that the drunk passed out, sleeping through the rest of the flight, landing and arrival. Almost everyone was off the airplane, but the drunk snored on. Annoyed, the young flight attendant finally approached, shook his shoulder and told him that he had arrived.

Finally awake, the man smiled up at her and announced, "You know, I really would like to get in your pants."

With no hesitation, the woman looked him directly in the eyes and replied, "Thanks, but one asshole in these pants is quite enough!"

Flt 25

On preparing to return home from an out of town trip, a man got a small puppy as a present for his son. Not having time to get the paperwork to take the puppy on board, the man just hid the pup down the front of his pants and sneaked him on board the airplane.

About 30 minutes into the trip, a flight attendant noticed the man shaking and quivering. "Are you okay, sir?" "Yes," said the man, "but I have a confession to make. I didn't have time to get the paperwork to bring a puppy on board, so I hid him down the front of my pants."

"What's wrong? Is he not housebroken?"

"No, that's not the problem. The problem is he's not weaned yet!"

Flt 26

Another "Tale from the dark side" from a flight attendant . . .

There have been so many stories about "Casanova" pilots that it's become a cliche. The sad truth is that like smoke and fire, there's a lot to the stories. As just about any gal who's trod the aircraft aisles for a living can tell you, there are a lot of pilots who think that the ability to drive an airplane also makes them among the world's greatest lovers. While most are really nice guys, there are a fair share who must think they're God's gift to women and that flight attendants will swoon whenever they start to shovel their line of B.S.

Our misfortune on one trip was to spend several days crewed with one of these flying Romeo's. Though he was single, and not too hard to look at, every woman on the crew was fed up with his arrogant, cock-sure attitude. One of his favorite lines: "Hi, 'Sugar'. Why don't you call me by my first name . . . 'Captain'." The chance to take a guy like this down a notch or two doesn't come along too often, but on our last leg of the trip, Salt Lake City to New York, an opportunity presented itself.

Several of us had noticed a tall, striking woman board and take her seat in the first class cabin. She was immaculately dressed and manicured, looking for all the world like she was headed to a modeling session for "Cosmo" magazine. All of us gals were feeling frumpy by comparison until we had a chance to take a closer look and talk to her a bit during the rather elaborate dinner service. You guessed it. "She" wasn't a she at all, but a man who looked and dressed the part well enough to pass all but the closest inspection.

While taking coffee to the flight crew, I casually mentioned that we had a really striking passenger sitting in 3C. Immediately, the captain's radar came on, and I could see him trying to catch a glimpse of the beauty in the back as I opened the crew door to return to the cabin. We were all placing bets on how long it would take him to find a reason to come to the back, trying to suppress smiles as we went about our duties. Sure enough, it wasn't long before he left the cockpit to "use the restroom". After leaving the lavatory, he chatted with the two of us up front for a minute or two, but his eyes kept wandering toward the "lady" in 3C.

As casually as he could, he eased into the first class cabin, nodding and speaking to several of the passengers as he honed in on his target. Barely containing our laughter, we watched as Romeo started a conversation. By the time he was perched on the armrest, leaning closer for a more quiet chat with the passenger, I had to put a towel to my face to keep from laughing out loud. But I have to give Romeo's radar credit, after just a minute or two, the light bulb went on, and he realized he was talking sweetly to a *man*. He sat back suddenly like he'd been slapped, and though we couldn't hear what he said, started making a hasty retreat. At this point, my co-worker and I lost it. I'm sure you could hear our peals of laughter back in coach.

If looks could kill, I'd never have lived to tell this tale. The captain glared daggers at me as, red-faced, he hurried back into the cockpit. I've flown with this pilot since, and he's been a cool professional every time. And, he's never again called me "Sugar".

Flt 27
From an flight attendant: "Welcome aboard ACE Flight 781 to Houston. To operate your seatbelt,

insert the metal tab into the buckle and pull tight. It works just like every other seatbelt, so if you don't know how to operate one, you probably shouldn't be out in public unsupervised. In the event of a sudden loss of cabin pressure, oxygen masks will descend from the ceiling. Stop screaming, grab the mask and pull it over your face. If you have a small child traveling with you, secure your mask before assisting with theirs. If you are traveling with two small children, decide now which one you love more. For our passengers who smoke, you will find our smoking section conveniently located on the left wing. Federal law prohibits tampering with, destroying or disabling a smoke detector. If you tamper with the detectors, you will be relocated to the smoking section. Thank you, and remember, nobody loves you or your money more than ACE."

Flt 28

Ace Airlines FA: "Ladies and Gentlemen, as you are all now painfully aware, our Captain has landed in Seattle. From all of us at Ace Airlines, we'd like to thank you for flying with us today. Please be very careful as you open the overhead bins as you may be killed by falling luggage that has shifted during our so-called touchdown.

Flt 29

About five or six years ago I was on a flight into Amarillo, Texas, on a particularly windy and bumpy day. I could tell during the final approach that the

Captain was really having to fight it, and after an extremely hard landing, the Flight Attendant came on the P.A. and announced, "Ladies and Gentleman, welcome to Amarillo. Please remain in your seats with your seatbelt fastened while the Captain taxis what's left of our MD-80 to the gate!"

Flt 30

Another flight attendant's comment on a less than perfect landing: "We ask you to remain seated as Captain Kangaroo bounces us to the terminal!"

Flt 31

P.A. announcement from a young pilot: "Sorry about the rough landing, folks. I'm still practicing. Next time I'll try to lose your luggage."

Flt 32

"As we prepare for takeoff, please make sure your tray tables and seat backs are fully upright in their most uncomfortable position."

Flt 33

"There may be 50 ways to leave your lover, but there are only 4 ways out of this airplane."

Flt 34

"Your seat cushions can be used for floatation, and in the event of an emergency water landing, please take them with our compliments."

Flt 35

"Smoking in the lavatories is prohibited. Any person caught smoking in the lavatories will be asked to leave the plane immediately."

Flt 36

"Good morning. As we leave Dallas, it's warm, the sun is shining, and the birds are singing; however, we are going to Charlotte, where it's dark, windy and raining. Why in the world y'all wanna go there, I really don't know!"

Flt 37

Pilot: "Folks, we have reached our cruising altitude now, so I am going to switch the seat belt sign off. Feel free to move about as you wish, but please stay inside the plane 'til we land. It's a bit cold outside, and if you walk on the wings it affects the aircraft's flight characteristics."

Flt 38

Pilot: "Folks, if you were with us last week, we never got around to mentioning that it was National Procrastination Day. If you get a chance this week, please try to celebrate it. If you can't get to it, then maybe try to do it over the weekend, but no big rush. Have a nice day."

Flt 39

And, after landing: "Thank you for flying ACE Business Express. We hope you enjoyed giving us the business as much as we enjoyed taking you for a ride."

Flt 40

As we waited just off the runway for another airliner to cross in front of us, some of the passengers were beginning to retrieve luggage from the overhead bins. The head steward announced on the intercom, "This aircraft is equipped with a video surveillance system that monitors the cabin during taxiing. Any passengers not remaining in their seats until the aircraft comes to a full and complete stop at the gate will be strip-searched as they leave the aircraft.

Flt 41
As the plane landed and was coming to a stop at Washington National, a lone voice came over the loudspeaker: "Whoa, big fella . . . WHOA!!"

Flt 42
"Should the cabin lose pressure, oxygen masks will drop from the overhead area. Please place the bag over your own mouth and nose before assisting children or adults acting like children."

Flt 43
"As you exit the plane, please make sure to gather all of your belongings. Anything left behind will be distributed evenly among the flight attendants. Please do not leave children or spouses."

Flt 44
And from the pilot during his welcome message: "We are pleased to have some of the best flight attendants in the industry. Unfortunately none of them are on this flight."

Flt 45
On a flight to the Virgin Islands, the cabin crew was going through the monotony of the pre-departure safety briefing. They got the usual amount of attention-- which is to say, none at all,

until one gal got several others together. They donned their diving equipment -- mask, snorkel and fins . . . and continued with the "over water" portion of the briefing. Needless to say, they got every passenger's attention and a round of applause.

Flt 46

A veteran flight attendant tells us that in the 80's, flights were loaded with hard working, hard drinking Texans on their way to and from the oil fields. She recalls one flight that was being served in the back by identical twin sisters. A ruddy driller stopped Twin #1 and asked her for a scotch and water. A few minutes later, Twin #2 passed by. He hailed her and asked, "Hey, Little Lady. Where's my drink?" Looking confused, Twin #2 replied that she didn't know he wanted a drink. At that moment Twin #1 appeared, holding his scotch and water. Looking back and forth at the sisters, the Texan exclaimed, "No thanks, I gotta stop drinkin!"

Flt 47

The same attendant remembers another Texas oil man who ordered a Jack Daniel's and milk on an early bird flight to Midland-Odessa. Not sure she'd heard correctly, she repeated, "A Jack Daniel's and MILK?" "Yep. My doctor tells me I've got a doggoned ulcer, and I'm supposed to drink milk."

Flt 48

A flight attendant reports that she will be more

careful with safety briefings in the future, as some passengers will apparently believe anything . . .

The flight attendant spiced up her safety briefing by adding some humor when she got to the part about smoking restrictions. She announced that those passengers wishing to smoke would find the smoking section located over the left and right wings. She continued, "For those of you wishing to use our outdoor patio smoking area, you will encounter some strong winds, so please make use of the parachute you'll find under your seat, and remember to hold on tight!"

Shortly after this announcement the attendant noticed a woman sitting in her seat with a life preserver on. She told the passenger, "Ma'am, the life jackets are to be used only in case of an emergency." Looking confused, the woman replied, "Life jacket? I thought this was a parachute. I was just going out for a smoke."

Flt 49
From a flight attendant . . .

While working a beverage service on a flight from L.A. to Honolulu, I was stopped by a passenger who informed me that he had seen a snake slither by underneath his seat.

Thinking the man had had one Mai Tai too many,

I played along and asked if he knew where the snake was. He said he wasn't sure, but pointed to a row of seats and told me that he had last seen the critter headed in that direction.

Trying to maintain what little dignity I could, I crawled down the aisle, looking between passengers' legs and under the seats. Sure enough, there was a fairly large snake meandering through the airplane, unnoticed by the passengers. Unnoticed, that is until my scream all but broke the wine glasses on the beverage cart.

In the ensuing pandemonium, with passengers and flight attendants scrambling to get away from the serpent, the copilot bravely captured the beast, bagged him in a garbage bag, and threw it into the lavatory for safekeeping. Fortunately, the in-flight movie for the day was NOT "Anaconda."

Flt 50
A flabbergasted flight attendant watched with amusement as a female passenger pushed the attendant call button and, apparently thinking that the device worked like a McDonald's drive-through, loudly asked, "Excuse me, can I get a cup of coffee?"

Flt 51
Submitted by a flight attendant . . ."While boarding

soldiers on a flight from Saudi, Arabia, there was one young man who simply took my breath away. The word gorgeous was just the beginning in describing him. During the flight we engaged in small talk and I found myself wanting more than anything to make his flight as comfortable as possible. I found a center row of seats in the aft of the 747 that was unoccupied and offered that section to him so that he could lay down and relax. He accepted. I quickly gathered up all the extra pillows and blankets I could find and made him a bed. Later, I went to check on him and noticed that he looked a bit uncomfortable, so I offered to fluff his pillows. As he lifted his hand to rise, I was horrified to see that he was wearing a WEDDING BAND! I immediately snatched all the pillows from under him and let his head hit the armrest. How dare he lead me on!"

Flt 52

Ninety minutes before the flight from London landed in New York, its cabin lights were turned on so the flight attendants could serve breakfast. One of the passengers, upset because he was awakened, growled, "Who turned on the f...ing lights?"

"Oh, no sir.", the nearest flight attendant replied sweetly. "Those are the breakfast lights. You slept right through the f...ing lights."

Turb 1

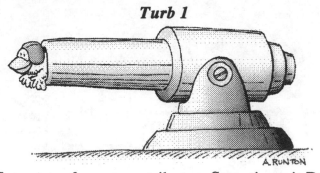

True story from a contributor: Sometimes it DOES take a Rocket Scientist . . .

Scientists at NASA have developed a gun built specifically to launch dead chickens at the windshields of airliners, military jets, and the space shuttle all traveling at maximum velocity. The idea is to simulate the frequent incidents of collisions with airborne fowl to test the strength of the windshields.

British engineers heard about the gun and were eager to test it on the windshields of their new high speed trains. Arrangements were made. But, when the gun was fired, the engineers stood shocked as the chicken hurled out of the barrel, crashed into the shatterproof shield, smashed it to smithereens, continued through the control console, snapped the engineer's backrest in two and embedded itself in the back wall of the cabin. Horrified Britons sent NASA the disastrous results of the experiment, along with the designs of the windshield, and begged the U.S. scientists for suggestions.

NASA sent back a very official looking one-line report that read: "Thaw the chicken."

Turb 2

We had an overnight in D.C. with an early departure for the airport at 5:30 am. The whole crew was waiting in the lobby, less the new (blonde) flight attendant. Finally, at 5:35, I decided to give her room a call to find out what the hold up was. She answered the phone! I said, "What are you doing? We're all in the lobby ready to leave! You're late!" She answered, "I know, but I'm trapped in my room!" "How can you be trapped in your room?", I asked. "Well," she said, "there are only two doors; one is to the bathroom and the other has a "Do Not disturb" sign on it."

Turb 3

Did you hear about the flight attendant that was so dumb that the other two noticed?

Turb 4

A veteran airline captain, apparently checking in with air traffic control on the wrong frequency, was asked, "Say your position?" To which he replied, "Captain".

Turb 5

According to a long-time flight attendant, a male pilot is a confused soul who talks about women the whole time he's flying, and talks about flying whenever he's with a woman!

Turb 6

Another flight attendant asks, "How many airline pilots does it take to change a light bulb?" "Just one. He grabs it and waits for the world to revolve around him.

Turb 7

A. RUNTON

The controller working a busy pattern told the 727 on downwind to make a three-sixty (do a complete circle, usually to provide spacing between aircraft). The pilot of the 727 complained, "Do you know it costs us two thousand dollars to make a three-sixty in this airplane?" Without missing a beat the controller replied, "Roger, give me four thousand dollars worth!"

Turb 8

PSA was following an ACE Airlines flight, taxing out for departure. PSA called the tower and said "Tower, this is ACE 586. We've got a little problem, so go ahead and let PSA go first". The tower promptly cleared PSA for takeoff before ACE crew had a chance to object to the impersonation!

Turb 9

A DC-10 had an exceedingly long landing rollout after landing with his approach speed just a little too high. San Jose Tower: "ACE 751 Heavy, turn right at the end if able. If not able, take the first exit off of Highway 101 back to the airport."

Turb 10
During a very busy departure rush at Kennedy airport, the following exchange was heard on the tower frequency:

Unknown Aircraft: "I'm f--king bored!"

Tower: "Last aircraft transmitting, identify yourself immediately!"

Unknown Aircraft: "I said I was f--king bored, not f--king stupid!"

Turb 11
Here's a few of the buttons you might find if you look on the *inside* of crew coats:

"People like you should ride the bus!" - for obnoxious passengers.

"Check your brains with your baggage?" - for the ditzy passenger.

"If you want to fly the Friendly Skies - sit down and shut up until we get there!"

Turb 12
Responding to a reported fire in the galley of an airliner sitting at the gate being made ready for departure, the airport's fire department pulled up to the side of the aircraft and shot huge quantities of fire suppressant foam into the open passenger door. What the firemen couldn't see, due to the thick smoke pouring out of the galley area, was the open

service door on the oppoiste side of the airplane. The foam was simply shooting in one door and out the other, onto the ramp. While no one was on board, and there were no injuries, the aircraft was a total loss.

Turb 13

The German controllers at Frankfurt Airport are a short-tempered lot. They not only expect transient pilots to know their parking location, but how to get there without any assistance from them. So it was with some amusement that we (PanAm 747) listened to the following exchange between Frankfurt ground and a British Airways 747 (radio call Speedbird 106) after landing:

Speedbird 206: "Good morning Frankfurt, Speedbird 206 clear of the active."
Ground: "Guten morgan, taxi to your gate."
The British Airways 747 pulls on the the main taxiway and stops.
Ground: "Speedbird 206, do you not know where you are going?"
Speedbird 206: "Stand by, ground, I'm looking up the gate location now."
Ground (with typical German impatience): "Speedbird 206, have you never flown to Frankfort before?"
Speedbird 206 (coolly): "Yes, in 1944. But I didn't stop.

Turb 14

A recent newspaper article about events on an Aeroflot Airlines flight brings out some of the differences in travel on the Russian carrier.

According to the article, several passengers reported the same bizarre events aboard the flight. A pilot was 40 minutes late for departure, and was spat upon by a flight attendant, who called him a drunk. The incensed pilot refused to start the engines, yelling from the cockpit that the plane wouldn't leave until the flight attendant apologized. Several irate passengers threatened to kill the pilot.

During the flight, a woman's St. Bernard puppy, riding in her lap threw up. Several chickens escaped from the overhead and ran through the aisle, avoiding attempts to recapture them.

Commenting on this story, an Aeroflot official was quoted as saying the carrier was making serious attempts to improve the airline's image. He reported a program to paint the aircraft in the fleet and outlined recent improvements in service. For example, employees have been told that there will be no more stealing of luggage.

The Russian official stated, "We're trying to be like the U.S. airlines."

Here are some actual maintenance complaints submitted by pilots, and the replies from the maintenance crews.

Problem: Left inside tire almost needs replacement.
Solution: Almost replaced left inside tire.

Problem. Test flight OK, except Autopilot Autoland feature very rough.
Solution: Autopilot Autoland feature not installed on this aircraft.

Problem: Something loose in cockpit.
Solution: Something tightened in cockpit.

Problem: Evidence of hydraulic leak on right main landing gear.
Solution: Evidence removed.

Problem: Radio volume unbelievably loud.

Solution: Radio volume set to a more believable level.

Problem: Dead bugs on windshield.
Solution: Live bugs on order.

Problem: Autopilot altitude hold produces a 200 ft. per minute descent.
Solution: Could not duplicate problem on ground.

Problem: Number 2 radio inoperable.
Solution: Number 2 radio inoperable in "OFF" mode.

Problem: Number 3 engine is missing.
Solution: Number 3 engine found on right wing.

Turb 16

We've recently heard rumors from airline folks of upcoming mergers or start-up airlines. While not claiming any truth to these rumors, we pass them on for what they're worth . . a laugh.

Federal Express (FedEx) merging with United Parcel Services (UPS)? The new package company would be called "FED-UP"

A new, all female company being formed by former employees of UPS? The company will be called "UPMS", and you'll get your package when they're damned good and ready.

Virgin Airlines and EasyJet combining to form "Easy Virgin"?

Fairchild Aircraft Manufacturing and Honeywell Electronics unite to create a new production company, "Fairwell Honeychild"?

Turb 17

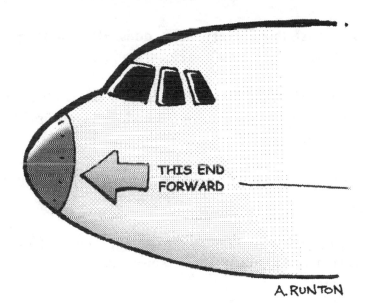

A. RUNTON

Pilot Wisdom:

It's better to be down here wishing you were up there, than to be up there wishing you were down here.

Any pilot who does not at least privately consider himself the best in the business is in the wrong business.

The only time you have too much fuel is when you're on fire.

The only thing worse than a captain who never flew copilot is a copilot who was once a captain.

Takeoffs are optional. Landings are mandatory.

The first thing every pilot does after making a gear up landing is to put the gear handle down.

A "good" landing is one which you can walk away from. A great landing is one which lets you use the airplane another time.

A good simulator check ride is like successful surgery on a cadaver.

Good judgment comes from experience. Good experience comes from someone else's bad judgment.

An airplane may disappoint a good pilot, but it won't surprise him.

Learn from the mistakes of others. You won't live long enough to make them all yourself.

An airplane will probably fly a little bit overweight, but it won't fly without fuel.

Speed is life, altitude is life insurance.

Never let an airplane take you somewhere your brain didn't get to five minutes earlier.

Too many pilots are found in the wreckage with their hands around a microphone or holding onto a keyboard. Don't drop the aircraft in order to fly the microphone . . . An airplane flies because of a principle discovered by Bernoulli, not Marconi.

Fly it until the last piece stops moving.

No one has ever collided with the sky.

Any attempt to stretch fuel is guaranteed to increase headwinds.

Keep looking around, there's always something you missed.

It's best to keep the pointed end going forward as much as possible.

Helicopters are for pilots who love to fly, but have no place to go.

Remember, you're always a student in an airplane.

Things which do you no good in aviation: Altitude above you. Runway behind you. Fuel in the truck. Half a second in history. Approach charts in the car. The airspeed you don't have.

A smooth touchdown in a simulator is about as exciting as kissing your sister.

Three things kill young pilots in Alaska: weather, weather, and weather.

Fuel is life . . Any captain who takes less than 45 minutes of holding fuel is playing Russian Roulette with the ground.

Turb 18
A pilot told us about overhearing an exchange on the approach control frequency between the controller and the pilot of a single engine military fighter. The pilot was requesting priority handling at a joint civil - military use airport due to a rough running engine. When the controller told this pilot he would be number 2 behind a B-52 (an **eight engine** bomber) with one engine shut down, the fighter jock commented dryly, "Ah, yes ,the dreaded seven-engine approach."

Turb 19
This one happened at a Navy training squadron in California. After landing, a new ensign wrote up this complaint about an A-7 that he just finished flying:

"Pilot relief tube too short." (The pilot relief tube is a device that allows a male pilot to relieve himself in flight if he's had a little too much coffee before climbing into the cockpit.)

When Maintenance investigated the "squawk" , they found that the relief tube was tangled around the base of the stick. After correcting the problem, they gave the pilot's chain (and probably his ego) a good yank by signing off the maintenance form like this: "Pilot relief tube found to be of sufficient length for enlisted personnel."

Turb 20
Airline pilots, like any of us, can have a tough time finding their way around an unfamiliar airport. One day at SJC (San Jose, CA), an ACE DC-10 was headed into unfamiliar territory. Controllers observed the aircraft come to a full stop just short of an intersecting taxiway and remain motionless. After a moment Ground Control called and said, "ACE 721 turn right at that taxiway." There was no response. Again the controller said, "ACE 721 turn right at that taxiway." No response. After a few seconds, the controller tried a different approach: "ACE 721, turn toward the copilot", at which point the aircraft made an immediate 90-degree turn to the right . . .

Turb 21
(API) A small two-seater Cessna 152 plane

crashed into a cemetery early this afternoon in central Poland. Search and Rescue workers have recovered 300 bodies so far, and expect that number to climb as digging continues into the evening.

Turb 22

A young student pilot was flying his single engine trainer on a solo flight. Putting along, lost in the scenery, he began to realize that none of that scenery looked familiar. After checking his maps and making several turns to locate something to fix his position, he came to the unpleasant realization that he was lost.

Trying not to panic, he considered his options. Consulting his charts, he located the correct radio frequency for the Air Traffic Control Center in the general area. After several attempts, he succeeded in contacting a controller and explained his predicament.

Following established procedure for the situation, the controller first tried to get some point of reference by asking, "What was your last known position?" "Sir", the student meekly replied, "I guess that would be when I taxied onto the runway for takeoff!"

Glossary of Terms

Flight Schedule: An entertaining work of paperback fiction.

On Time: An obscure term, meaning unknown.

Delayed: Situation Normal.

New Departure Time: We haven't got a clue.

Mechanical Hold: Looking for the instruction book.

Weather Hold: We're trying to decide "weather" or not to go.

Air Traffic Control: A government agency funded by the airlines. Major function: to be blamed for all departure and arrival delays.

Fog: A natural weather phenomenon which usually occurs around an airport while the surrounding areas are clear. Fog is controlled by the airlines and is used to delay flights.

Baggage Claim: The most difficult area of the airport to find. It is usually hidden by numerous signs saying, "Baggage Claim Area".

Position Closed: This is a sign posted at most counter locations, which interpreted by the passenger says, "Form line here".

Passenger: A herding creature of widely varying intellect, usually found in pairs or small groups. Often will become vicious or violent in simple, rectifiable situations.

No Record: Any passenger booked through a travel agent.

Carry-on Bag: An item, usually of large dimensions, which somehow manage to fit under the passenger's seat on the inbound flight, but cannot be crammed into the same space on the return.....

In-Flight Meal: Peanuts.

In Flight Meal (1st Class): Choice of peanuts or pretzels.

First Class: The part of the airplane where you turn your head and smell leather instead of armpit.

Safety Briefing: The in-flight movie that nobody hears or sees.

Information
Counter: A location at an airport where passengers congregate to ask questions such as: "What time does my flight depart?" .....
"WHEN?!!!"
"Where am I going?"
"Where is the information counter?"

In-Flight
Announcement: A vital communication of safety information, delivered over loudspeakers formerly used (and rejected) by fast food drive-through windows.

Pillows & Blankets: Items provided by airlines for passenger comfort. Purchased from hospital pre-natal care wards when they are rejected for being too small.

Pilot: The person who sits in front of
                        the airplane. A highly trained
                        professional whose primary
                        duties consist of making
                        in-flight announcements (see
                        above). Announcements usually
                        begin right after you've fallen
                        asleep or during the middle of
                        the in-flight movie. Pilots can
                        be identified off duty by their
                        incredibly large wristwatches
                        and sunglasses so dark they
                        require a seeing-eye dog.

Co-Pilot: The second person who sits in
                        front of the airplane. Primary
                        consist of handling radio
                        communications ("Was that for
                        us?") and standing near the exit
                        upon arrival to accept the
                        passengers' glares after a hard
                        landing.

Flight Attendant: A safety specialist who protects
                        passengers from the hazards of
                        seats not being in their upright
                        and locked position.

Gate Agent: An airline employee who
                        conveys vital information to
                        passengers about flights that are

late arriving, late leaving, cancelled or moved to another gate.

Baggage Handler: Gorilla.

Thunderstorm: Nature's way of saying "Up yours."

Weather Forecast: A horoscope with numbers.

AIR
SICK
HUMOR
TWO

Heard one . . . Seen one?
Please Share.

If you fly fairly regularly, you may have seen some things yourself that made you shake your head in wonder. If you'd like to share these stories, pass them on to Bill:

Air Sick Humor
O &A, Inc.
P.O. Box 686
Sharpsburg, GA 30277
Fax: 770-502-9138
EMail: Billjoric@aol.com